After-School
◆ ◆
Transition
◆
Activities

THE READY SET GO!

Guide To Strategies That Work

by David L. Whitaker

School-Age NOTES ● **Nashville, TN**

David L. Whitaker has worked in child care since 1987 as lead teacher, program coordinator, trainer and consultant. He has worked with all ages of children in a variety of program settings including preschool, kindergarten, before-and-after school programs and summer programs. In 1998 David formed Toolbox Training in response to the increasing demand for tools by which to improve the quality of child care. He has developed over a dozen training packages which he uses in his workshops. Titles include *Discipline with Dignity* and *Connect with Families: The K.I.D.S. Method*. David has served on the Missouri School-Age Care Coalition and the Missouri Accreditation state board. He has a Bachelor of Arts degree in Speech Communication and a Masters in Education. He currently lives in the Kansas City, MO with his wife, Becky and their son Evan.

Other titles by **David L. Whitake**r include: *Games, Games, Games: Creating Hundreds of Group Games & Sports, Multiple Intelligences & After-School Environments: Keeping All Children in Mind,* and *In Pursuit of NSACA Accreditation.*

For more information on **Toolbox Training** and workshops by David Whitaker:

TOOLBOX TRAINING
6121 Robinson, Overland Park, KS 66202
Phone: 913-789-9733
email: toolbox_training@yahoo.com
www.toolboxonline.bigstep.com

ISBN: 0-917505-16-6

10 9 8 7 6 5 4 3 2 1

© Copyright 2003. David L. Whitaker. All Rights Reserved

Published by School-Age NOTES, P.O. Box 40205, Nashville TN 37204

TABLE OF CONTENTS

Activities: Making Transitions Fun

INTRODUCTION

Why I Wrote This Book

As the world slowly recognizes the value of quality child care, more and more resources exist to help providers in offering the best programs possible. One can find numerous books detailing art projects, games, and any number of other kinds of activities.

There are resources designed to aide in the set up of new programs. There are resources to help child care staff plan daily schedules and master appropriate discipline techniques.

In short, the big picture has been extensively covered. What has been lost in the process, however, are the details.

I have yet to find a resource that helps child care staff in one of the most prominent parts of any child care program's schedule - the transition. Seemingly trivial and a necessary evil, transitions are usually overlooked as just those few moments of wait time during which children must get from here to there.

However, that wait time can become great time - if programs know how to take advantage of it.

This book will help in three ways. The first section focuses on evaluating daily transitions to decide which are effective and which are not. The second section provides tips on how to make transitions more effective. Finally, the third (and largest) section of the book offers activities ranging from games to songs that can be used to turn wait time into great time. Enjoy!

Ready...

Set...

Go!

Pump, Lump, or Dump:
Making Transitions Better

PUMP, LUMP, OR DUMP

The Joy of Waiting in Line: A Story

Travis, 11, and his sister Tara, 7, were in a before- and after-school program at their school. Among other activities, there was a circle time every afternoon. Sometimes they did group games or activities; sometimes they sang songs; sometimes they did planning.

On this particular day, the kids were asked to discuss some of their all-time favorite places to go. The discussion quickly turned toward amusement parks.

"Well," Tara piped up, "my favorite ride is that one that spins you around and you stick to the walls and then you feel like you're gonna throw up."

This evoked giggles from others, but also elicited other responses. Someone else said they liked the bumper cars. Another person favored "That one boat ride that goes down that big hill and splashes you and you get all wet."

The group all seemed in agreement about roller coasters. Those were definitely the most fun. The kids talked about how they got scared, how they held on or didn't hold on, and whether or not they liked the ones that went upside down.

Travis jumped in with a different observation. "You know, those rides are all fun, but there's one problem." The group was eager to hear what could possibly be wrong with an amusement park. "Well," he said, "you have to stand around in line and wait a lot."

A Definition

What is a transition? In the book *Half a Childhood, Quality Programs for Out-of-School Hours*, transitions are defined as "simply the change from one experience to another."[1] Within a given day, a school-ager experiences numerous transitions at home, school, and in an after-school program. Instead of being frustrated with their need to push the limits once they reach the after-school program, we should be startled that they manage to function at all with so many changes every day.

The average child experiences transitions at home when getting out of bed, cleaning up, getting dressed, eating breakfast, and heading to school. During the school day that child will experience numerous more changes as she is thrown into various subjects, goes to different rooms, heads to lunch, has recess, or even just goes to the bathroom.

This book, though, specifically focuses on the transitions a child experiences while in the after-school program. The next few pages will analyze the possible transitions a child might experience. This book then explores how transitions can be made as effective as possible. Finally, for transitions to be truly successful, they must be fun, so this book offers a treasure trove of easy-to-do transition activities.

Transitions:
the change from one experience to another.

[1]Bender, Judith, Charles H. Flatter and Jeanette M. Sorrentino. *Half a Childhood, Quality Programs for Out-of-School Hours.* 2nd edition, completely revised. 2000. Nashville: School-Age NOTES. (p. 231).

Guinea Pig Elementary

Guinea Pig Elementary's district-sponsored school-age program (GP-SAC) averages 45 children with three staff each morning and around 60 children and four staff members every afternoon.

The children have a wide range of materials to use and have daily access to the school's cafeteria, gymnasium, library, and computer lab. The program is also fortunate to be well supported by the families served and the staff in the school building.

GP-SAC has not always been top-notch, however. They once regularly fielded complaints from children, parents, and school staff about how disorganized the program was. The staff knew that the program didn't work; they were frustrated on a daily basis because the children were always restless and unfocused. They argued with each other and the adults. No one seemed to want to be there.

One of the staff members went to a workshop and left with a powerful message that she just couldn't shake: "Waiting is death." She told the rest of the staff about the phrase that was now stuck in her head. Slowly, the staff started to realize what was killing their program. The kids were doing a lot of waiting.

Once they realized that, the GP-SAC program evaluated their daily schedules. They looked at how many transitions they were making kids go through each day. They looked at how inconsistent they were from day to day in their schedules. They looked at which transitions were vital and which weren't. Slowly but surely, they found ways to streamline their schedules and make the necessary transitions fun, quick, and painless.

Today the school, the parents, the staff, and the children are all much happier. Things run smoothly and there are few complaints. The children are more focused and have fewer problems. The SAC staff have posted their new motto where they will see it every day and be reminded of the program's transformation: "Waiting is death."

The PFPF Rule

When the staff from GP-SAC started evaluating their daily schedule and the transitions, they developed four standards by which to judge each component of the day. They called it the **PFPF** rule.

PURPOSE:

What is the purpose of the transition? Is it serving that purpose? Is this transition absolutely necessary?

FUN:

Are the kids enjoying it?

PACE:

How long is the transition? Is it too fast or too slow?

FLEXIBILITY:

Is the transition too rigid or too relaxed? Do children have enough say (or too much) in what's going on?

PUMP, LUMP, OR DUMP

3 Ways to Fix Transitions That Don't Work

After they used the PFPF rule to evaluate the transitions in their daily schedule, the GP-SAC staff fixed their problems with three different methods:

PUMP:

If the problem with a transition was that it was necessary but just boring, then the staff found a way to jazz it up and make it more fun.

LUMP:

Sometimes the staff found that a transition could be combined with something else.

DUMP:

There were other times that the staff realized they didn't need a transition at all so they just completely scrapped it.

In some cases, the GP-SAC staff combined methods to fix a transition.

Guinea Pig's Morning Schedule

The GP-SAC staff went through their daily routine, dissecting every part of it by using the PFPF rule. When they started, their schedule looked like this:

OLD MORNING SCHEDULE
(Before evaluating with the PFPF rulle.)

6:30 Opening/Set Up   Staff arrive. Doors are opened for children to come in. Kids start helping staff set up materials.

6:30 Free Time   Children choose an area to play in.

6:45 Change Areas   Children switch to a new area.

7:00 Change Areas   Children switch to a new area.

7:15 Change Areas   Children switch to a new area.

7:30 Change Areas   Children switch to a new area.

7:45 Clean Up   Children clean up area and wait for adult to excuse them to bring toys to storage to put away. Children then line up at door.

8:00 Wash Hands   Once all areas are cleaned up and all children are lined up, everyone goes to wash hands for breakfast.

8:10 Breakfast   As children finish, they are to remain in their seats until the bell rings.

8:30 Dismissal   When bell rings, the adults will excuse the children as soon as their tables are quiet.

6:30 A.M.

Opening/Set Up

The PFPF Rule

Purpose: When the GP-SAC staff applied the PFPF rule to this part of the day, they immediately realized they were trying to accomplish two purposes at once – open and get set up.

Fun: The first kids who arrived came into an empty room. They had to help the adults set up materials. One of the first kids who arrived was always still sleepy and whined that he didn't want to do any work yet. Another child came in already pumped up and ready for action and she wasn't too happy about having to work at setting up the room before she could do anything.

Pace: Because staff were trying to greet parents and children as they set up the room, this process usually stretched out for awhile.

Flexibility: Children had very little control over this part of the day.

Pump, Lump, or Dump

The GP-SAC staff decided that it wasn't fair to expect kids to help set up. Kids should be able to come in and immediately choose an activity. The staff **dumped** that transition for the kids by opting to come in 15 minutes earlier and set up the room before kids arrived. This also **pumped** up the transition that children experienced upon arrival since they could immediately choose an activity.

Revised

6:15 A.M.

  Staff Arrival

6:30 A.M.

  Opening/Set Up

Areas and Free Time

The PFPF Rule

Purpose: Under the old schedule, children were able to choose areas when they arrived. However, every fifteen minutes children had to switch areas. The idea was that they would get a better variety of experiences than if they chose wherever they wanted to go. In re-evaluating the purpose behind this idea, the staff realized that children were very frustrated with not getting to spend as much (or as little) time as they wished in an area.

Fun: Because children had no say regarding how long they could spend in areas, they weren't having a lot of fun. They wanted to be able to go to whichever areas they wanted for however long they wanted.

Pace: Obviously pace was a problem. The fifteen minutes that children had to spend in areas were not conducive to a child who wanted to become more involved in a project or a child who changed his mind.

Flexibility: The approach of regular rotating proved to be overly rigid for the children.

Pump, Lump, or Dump

The GP-SAC staff completely **dumped** the idea that children had to rotate every fifteen minutes. Instead, as children arrived they could choose whichever areas they wished and spend as long as they wanted there.

Revised
6:30 A.M. -8:15 A.M.
Free Time/
Breakfast

Clean Up and Five-Minute Warning

The PFPF Rule

Purpose: As the morning concludes, the staff need the children to help clean up materials. In the old schedule it was necessary to get everything picked up so that the whole group could then eat breakfast.

Fun: This proved to be a problem for several reasons. While the kids needed to help clean up and bring materials to adults to put in storage, it wasn't a lot of fun for them to wait until they were called on to bring their materials to the adult.

Pace: This process went very slowly because the children did not want to stop what they were doing and clean up. Because they knew they were going to have to wait if they got cleaned up first, this slowed down their desire to clean up even more.

Flexibility: Children resented that they all had to stop what they were doing and they all had to clean up and then wait. This system gave the children too little flexibility.

Pump, Lump, or Dump

The clean up was **lumped** in with two new pieces that the staff decided to add to their schedule - five-minute warnings and gatherings.

The five-minute warning was given each day to let the kids know that free time was coming to an end. When it was announced that it was time to clean up, then the children were responsible for putting away what they used and tidying up their areas. Once that was done, they could go directly to gathering (more on that later) instead of waiting. Each week, the staff asked for a couple of children to volunteer as clean-up helpers. Those children then brought materials to the adults to put away as soon as an area was cleaned up.

Wash Hands and Breakfast

The PFPF Rule

Purpose: Breakfast was provided for all children every morning. Staff members were careful to make sure all children washed hands before eating breakfast.

Fun: Since all the children had to wait for clean up to be finished, then all go together to wash hands, and then all eat breakfast, there was very little fun involved. The kids didn't like having to wait, move as a group, and being forced to sit at the breakfast tables even if they didn't want to eat.

Pace: A definite pattern was emerging in the transition problems. Everything was moving too slowly! The hand-washing and breakfast transition was especially slow because it involved several steps.

Flexibility: The children had no choice about eating breakfast, which was frustrating to those children who already ate or didn't like what was being served. There was also another problem - the children who arrived at 6:30 and wanted to eat breakfast were starved by the time they got to eat over an hour and a half later. The other problem with breakfast was that some children ate quickly and had to sit there and wait while other children couldn't finish their breakfast before the bell rang.

Pump, Lump, or Dump

The GP-SAC staff **lumped** breakfast with free time. This solved a number of problems. Breakfast was now something that children could choose. They still had to wash hands before they could eat, but now the children did not have to line up, wait for everyone else, and then go wash hands as one large group. They could decide if they wanted breakfast or not and if they ate they could take as long as they wanted and eat what they wanted.

Revised
8:20 A.M.
   Gathering

Gathering

The PFPF Rule

Purpose: This was a new piece that the GP-SAC staff added to eliminate some of the waiting that children had to do during clean up and breakfast times.

Fun: Once the clean-up process was simplified and breakfast time lumped in with free time, then the staff had to determine how to keep the children from waiting for the bell to ring after they cleaned up. They decided to add a **gathering**, or circle time, that children could join as they cleaned up. In gathering, the children would have opportunities for sharing or participation in group activities.

Pace: The immediate concern was how to keep children from having to wait for **gathering** to officially begin. It was decided that as soon as the first child was cleaned up and ready for gathering, an adult would get it started. The activity had to be something that other children could easily join as they arrived.

Flexibility: This approach allowed for a great deal of flexibility. It became okay to clean up quickly because the children knew they wouldn't have to sit and wait afterward. On the other hand, children who had more to pick up were given more flexibility with time so that they could get the job done without making others wait on them.

Pump, Lump, or Dump

The gathering was clearly a chance to **pump** up the last part of the morning schedule that usually dragged on because of all the waiting kids had to do. Now kids could be actively engaged in activity right up until time to go to class.

**8:30 A.M. -
Dismissal**

The New Morning Schedule

After they evaluated and revamped their morning schedule, the Guinea Pig SAC staff had eliminated some transitions, combined some, and jazzed up others. Their new schedule looks like this:

REVISED MORNING SCHEDULE
(After evaluating with the PFPF rule.)

6:15 Staff Arrival	Set up room and prepare for morning.
6:30 Opening/Set Up	Doors are opened for children to come in.
6:30 Free Time/ Breakfast	Children choose their own areas to to go to, including breakfast.
8:15 Five-Minute Warning	Children are told they have five more minutes.
8:20 Clean Up	Children pick up toys in their areas or finish activity.
8:20 Gathering	As children finish cleaning, they come to group time.
8:30 Dismissal	When bell rings, children are released to go to class.

Everyone was very pleased with how much smoother the mornings went. Children, the SAC staff, parents, and school staff were all much happier.

Guinea Pig's Afternoon Schedule

Before they evaluated and improved it, the afternoon schedule looked like this:

OLD AFTERNOON SCHEDULE
(Before evaluating with PFPF rule.)

3:15 Staff Arrival	Staff prepare snack.
3:30 Check In	Kids arrive and sit in designated rows to wait until everyone arrives and can be checked in by roll call.
4:00 Wash Hands/ Snack	All children go to wash hands and then come to snack together.
4:45 Outdoor Time	All children go outdoors to play. Time varies on the weather.
5:15 Restrooms/ Drinks	On the way inside, all children stop at the restrooms and get drinks.
5:30 Indoor Time	When all children are done with the restrooms and drinks, then the children that are left may choose a toy to get out from the storage cabinets. They will put the toys away as they go home.
6:00 Closing	Staff put away any remaining materials and go home.

There was much work to be done…

Staff Set Up

The PFPF Rule

Purpose: Staff were originally all scheduled to arrive just a few minutes beforehand since all that needed to be done was set up snack. The staff changed that idea, deciding instead to arrive earlier and set up the room with the free time materials.

Fun: Since only snack was available when children arrived, there was nothing else to do. Because of the lengthy check-in process, snack also sat out for a while before kids could have it. That meant warm things were cold and cold things were warm.

Pace: Of course, the adults were able to chat for a bit as soon as snack was set up and they liked that. They knew, however, that the rest of the afternoon was going to drag on because of all the wait time.

Flexibility: Because staff only set up snack, there was no flexibility in the children's routine. The staff realized that the children needed a definite routine, but that they needed some variety within that routine.

Pump, Lump, or Dump

By coming in just 15 minutes earlier, staff had time to set up the same areas and materials as they used in the mornings. This **pumped** up the afternoon program incredibly since it gave children something to do as soon as they arrived.

**Revised
3:00 P.M.**

Check In

The PFPF Rule

Purpose: The GP-SAC staff definitely thought it was crucial to be sure they had all children checked in each day. The rows and roll call approach let them be sure all children were accounted for, but...

Fun: The children hated it. Sitting in rows was boring and the children got very restless with nothing to do. Usually there was some kind of argument or altercation before all the kids even arrived. At the very least, staff found themselves constantly reminding children that they were supposed to sit down, not run around the room.

Pace: Because roll was not taken until all children arrived, there was a lot of waiting. Adults spent a lot of time telling children that if they would sit down and be quiet, this process would be much faster. It never worked; check in always ran about a half hour.

Flexibility: There was no flexibility in this approach. Children were expected to do what adults told them and there was not supposed to be any variance.

Pump, Lump, or Dump

The staff realized that they could not eliminate check in, but that they had to seriously revamp their approach. The waiting was killing the kids and the staff; there was a desperate need to **pump** up that transition. By the time they evaluated the rest of the schedule, they realized how much waiting the kids were doing and how little playing. They changed the check-in system so that kids simply came in and checked in with the adult who had the clipboard and then went straight to areas of their choice.

Snack

The PFPF Rule

Purpose: The GP-SAC program prided itself on offering children breakfast in the mornings and snack in the afternoons. They realized that children needed something to eat after school.

Fun: Of course, the staff reached the same conclusion regarding snack in the afternoons that they reached regarding breakfast in the mornings. The kids didn't like waiting, moving as a group, and being forced to sit at the snack tables even if they didn't want to eat.

Pace: Like the breakfast transition in the mornings, the snack transition just didn't work because it made kids sit and wait so much.

Flexibility: The children in the afternoon were as frustrated as those in the morning that they had no choice but to sit at the snack tables. The kids who finished first had to wait; the children who were slower usually didn't get enough time to eat.

Pump, Lump, or Dump

The GP-SAC staff **lumped** snack in with afternoon free time, just as they had lumped breakfast in with the morning free time. This solved a number of problems. Children could choose whether or not they wanted snack and could spend as little or as much time there as they wished. As in the mornings, children had to wash hands before eating snack, but they did not have to go as one large group.

Revised
3:30 - Wash
    Hands & Snack

4:45 P.M.

Outdoor Free Time

The PFPF Rule

Purpose: The staff thought it was important for children to have time to play outdoors.

Fun: Of course, it wasn't much fun for the children who really preferred to play inside. This especially became a problem in questionable weather when kids that didn't want to be too cold or too hot complained about having to be outside.

Pace: The pace was mostly a problem regarding how long it took to get outside - about an hour and fifteen minutes passed before kids got to go outside. This was torturous to those children who had a great need to burn off energy immediately after school.

Flexibility: The staff were at least flexible on time that children spent outdoors. They were not, however, flexible about children getting to choose whether or not they wanted to play outdoors.

Pump, Lump, or Dump

Revised
4:25 P.M.
5-Minute Warning

Once again, the GP-SAC staff saw an opportunity to **pump** up an unsuccessful transition, partially by moving it up on the schedule and also by **dumping** the notion that everyone had to go outside. Under the new schedule, as soon as kids arrived they had the option of snack, indoor free time, or outdoor free time.

Wash Hands/Restrooms/Drinks

5:15 P.M.

The PFPF Rule

Purpose: It certainly was necessary for children to wash hands before eating and have opportunities to use the restroom and get drinks; however...

Fun: These were agonizing transitions for children because everyone had to do them together as a group .

Pace: It didn't help that not everyone needed to go to the bathroom or get a drink at the same time. Still, because so many children were waiting, this process took a long time. Coming in from outside and stopping at the restrooms and drinking fountains took at least 15 minutes.

Flexibility: Children were allowed to go to the bathroom or get drinks at other times, so the staff realized that they could give up the idea that all kids needed to go at once.

Pump, Lump, or Dump

The staff completely **dumped** the bathroom/drinks transition. They let kids go when they needed to go. In regards to handwashing, children were simply expected to wash hands before getting a snack if they chose to eat snack.

Revised
4:30- 4:45 P.M.
    Cleanup
    Gathering
    Activity Time

5:30 P.M.

Indoor Free Time

The PFPF Rule

Purpose: Under the old schedule, there was only about 30 minutes for children to actually just play with the materials of their choice since check-in, snack, outdoor time, and restroom transitions took up so much time. The staff wanted children to have more time to play, but the transitions just took up so much time.

Fun: The staff were tired of children constantly asking when they could get the toys out. Surprise, surprise - the kids wanted to play more than they wanted to sit and wait.

Pace: The pace for getting to indoor free time had obviously been incredibly slow. Once children finally had opportunities for free time indoors, there was very little time left to play.

Flexibility: Because of the limited time, staff had no desire to completely set up the room with all of the materials and areas that they set up in the mornings. Children still had the flexibility to be able to ask for materials, but they were limited as to what they were allowed to have since adults didn't want to get out anything that would take long to clean up.

Pump, Lump, or Dump

The staff **pumped** up indoor free time by moving it to the beginning of the afternoon. That meant staff would set up the areas and materials beforehand. Children also had the option of playing indoors or outdoors and could choose to eat snack during this time if they wished.

<u>Revised</u>
5:15-6:00 P.M.
Free Time Until
Closing

The New Afternoon Schedule

The revamped afternoon schedule looked like this:

REVISED AFTERNOON SCHEDULE
(After evaluating with the PFPF rule.)

3:00 Staff Arrival	Staff set up room and prepare snack.
3:30 Check In	Kids check in and then choose indoor free time, snack, or outdoor free time.
3:30 Free Time	Children can go outdoors or stay indoors.
3:30 Wash Hands/ Snack	If children choose snack, they must go to the bathroom first to wash hands.
4:25 Five-Minute Warning	All children, indoors and out, receive a five-minute warning.
4:30 Cleanup	Children pick up materials and finish activities.
4:30 Gathering	As children finish cleaning, they come to gathering.
4:45 Activity Time	Children may choose from several scheduled afternoon activities.
5:15 Free Time- Inside	As children finish activities, they may return to indoor free time.
6:00 Closing	Staff put away any remaining materials and go home.

The staff added an afternoon gathering just as in the morning. They also added activity time in the afternoons so that part of the day was more spontaneous (free time) and part was more structured (activity time). Children choose from activities like games, art, science, drama, and music.

NOTES

Ready, Set, Go:
Making Transitions
Quick and Easy

READY, SET, GO!

3 Kinds of Transitions

Transitions can be divided into three categories:

READY . . .

These are transitions in which the adult(s) are trying to get all of the kids ready for the next part of the day. These are the typical "wait times" that occur when trying to get all of the kids shuffled through the bathroom or the line for the drinking fountain, or when changing clothes after swimming.

SET . . .

Once all of the kids are rounded up and in one place, they are waiting for what's to come. Circle times and gatherings of the entire group fit into this category as well as unexpected wait times, like waiting on a late field trip bus.

GO!

Now the kids are on the move from one activity to the next. This might be a transition from one room to another (such as taking a group to the gym) or from one activity to another.

Tips for Being Ready

When you are trying to get a group ready to do something else or move to a new activity, what are the best ways to make this happen?

1. **Avoid waiting.** Most of all, avoid waiting whenever possible. Children should not have to wait in lines to move from one activity to another, to go to the bathroom, to get drinks, etc.

2. **Adults should be prepared**. It isn't fair to expect children to wait because the adult isn't ready. That means the adult has all materials or supplies out and ready to use for activities.

3. **Get kids' help.** If it isn't possible for the adult to have everything ready, (such as measuring ingredients for a cooking project) then let kids help.

4. **Give five-minute warnings** to children before any activity switches. This gives them time to wrap up what they are doing.

Tips on Getting Set

Here are a few basic guidelines for establishing effective group times, circle times, and gatherings:

1. **If you have a daily scheduled group time, stick to this schedule.** Understandably the weather may cause you to extend or shorten your free time, but develop a set approach for such considerations with which both staff and kids are comfortable.

2. **Make five-minute warning and cleanup a regular part of the transition to scheduled group time.** If group time starts at 4:30, give kids a five minute warning at 4:25. At 4:30, start cleanup and make sure at least one adult is prepared to start group time as soon as the first child is finished.

3. **Put group time activities on a written schedule.** You will ensure more variety and eliminate the temptation to simply go with the first song that comes to mind – which also happens to be the same one you did yesterday, the day before, and the day before that. Having it in writing also allows the kids and adults to prepare for what's to come.

4. **Involve kids in leading group time.** It is important that the adults first establish a clear picture for the kids of what group time should look like, but once accomplished, kids should become part of the act. They can assist with or even lead songs and games. The adults can even give kids the option of signing up to be a group time helper or leader.

Note: See page 18 on "Gathering" in the PUMP, LUMP, OR DUMP section for better insight into the value of a daily, scheduled group time.

Getting Set: Questions About Group Time

What is group time? It can be called gathering or circle time or something else. Whatever the name, the intent should be the same – a time for the entire group to get together. It may be a time to meet, share, plan, discuss, or engage in an activity.

The kind of activity the group does may dictate the setting. For example, you may call your group time "circle time," but if kids are performing then the group may not be in the form of a circle at all. Do not let the terms get in the way of the objective.

Why have group time? Kids need an opportunity during each program day for a total group experience. This is a time for sharing, announcements, discussion of rules, explanations of the day's events and, quite simply, a time to get together. Children need various kinds of activity in an after-school program. They should have opportunities to participate in individual, small group, and total group experiences.

When should group time be? It is best sandwiched between free time and activity time. Because it is a time for announcements and explanations of the day's events, group time is an ideal time for introducing projects that will be offered later. To do that before free time means getting kids focused and settled down when their primary need is time to run and play outside, eat snack, be by themselves, chat with friends, or simply take a break at the end of a long school day and do nothing.

What about large groups? Group time does not necessarily consist of every child in the program. Once group size exceeds thirty kids, it is time to consider breaking groups down. With those kinds of numbers, a program should also have more than one space available to children.

However, if your program is housed in only one room or space, you may have several group times occurring simultaneously in different parts of the room. With multiple rooms, there might be a group time in each room.

How long should group time be? Group time should be viewed as a transition from free time to structured time in the afternoons and cleanup time to school time in the mornings. Cleanup time should be part of the daily routine in both the mornings and afternoons. As soon as kids begin cleaning up, adults should be ready to get children started on the group time activity. Do not make children sit and wait until everyone is done cleaning up because they will end up dreading group time. Get an activity started quickly and children will be encouraged to clean up quickly.

Once group time starts, it should continue until all children finish cleaning. Then the activity should be completed as soon as reasonably possible. Do not stop a game in the middle just because all the kids have arrived. Once the activity is done, make any necessary announcements and dismiss children to the next activity.

So what do we do during group time? A total group experience can pull from any of these categories, of which you will find activity suggestions in the next section of this book:

- Drama/Performance
- Games
- Guessing Games
- Group Creations
- Language
- Math and Science
- Music and Movement
- Planning
- Sharing

Tips to Get Going

When it is time to move from one space or activity to another, here are ways to make it as effective as possible:

1. **Avoid lines.** Kids are expected to move quietly in lines during the school day to avoid disrupting classes or other groups moving through the hallway. There is little or no need for this in a SAC program.

2. **Determine acceptable noise levels.** Are there other people in the building? What are acceptable indoor voices? Is there ever a need to move silently through the building?

3. **Face the kids.** If you are moving with a group of kids, then stay at the front and walk backwards so that you can see everyone. You could be at the back, but you have to make sure kids won't start racing each other to be in front.

4. **Be silly.** Kids hate walking down the hall in lines. Make the process fun!

5. **Provide variety.** Kids hate walking down halls and standing in lines because it has become so routine and was never fun in the first place. Make sure you give kids chances to have other more positive experiences.

NOTES

ACTIVITIES
Making Transitions Fun

READY . . .

SET. . .

GO!

ACTIVITIES

Introduction

There are all kinds of activities that can make transitions more fun. The activities in this book are divided into the following categories:

- Drama/Performance
- Games
- Guessing Games
- Group Creations
- Language

- Math and Science
- Music and Movement
- Planning
- Sharing

Each activity includes headings for "Materials" and "Directions." Most activities involve little or no materials since many transition times require spur-of-the-moment activities.

On a similar note, the "Directions" section is sparse to allow the reader to quickly access activities and grasp how to do them. Time is of the essence when one is working to make transitions fun and smooth.

Some of the activities also include a "Contributed by" heading. While this book started out with the tried-and-true activities I have done myself in programs, it quickly branched out to the ideas that others also have used. Thanks to everyone for your contributions!

Finally you will find the three figures on the cover of the book (and in the margin of this page) featured prominently throughout this section. While activities can usually be adapted to various kinds of transitions, the figure indicates the kind of transition for which the activity is best suited. Notice that certain categories fit certain kinds of transitions. For example, guessing games are good for "ready" transitions; drama and games are best for "set" transitions; music and movement works well on the "go."

Drama and Performance

When allowing children opportunities to perform, keep these guidelines in mind:

1. **Give children a set time frame** in which to work or they are inclined to soak up more spotlight than the audience may be willing to give.

2. **Require children to show performances to an adult first.** This makes kids responsible for preparing and allows an adult to evaluate appropriateness and length. When the actual performance occurs, adults can ensure that kids stick to the plan.

With that said, here's some suggestions for activities:

Act Out

Materials: story book(s)

Directions: One child or adult can read a story as others act it out. This might be more like a play where it has been practiced and prepared beforehand or it could be done impromptu with kids being picked to join in the story as new characters are introduced.

Band Performance

Materials: musical instruments (can be homemade)

Directions: Kids might give an air guitar performance or offer up a number with instruments provided by the site or made by the kids.

Charades

Materials: none

Directions: Kids can act out various movies, books, or TV shows for friends to guess.

Cheerleading

Materials: none

Directions: Kids can perform cheers for the group that have been learned or made up.

Dance to the Music

Materials: radio and/or tape/CD player with music CDs and/or tapes

Directions: Let kids dance to music. Some kids relish any opportunity to be a ham. Allowing children to get up and dance in front of a group can be very successful and entertaining. It is also interesting to have kids interpret different dance styles for different types of music. One child might switch the dial on the radio while other children dance accordingly. You can also let kids who take lessons perform what they have learned.

Lip Syncing

Materials: radio and/or tape/CD player with music CDs and/or tapes

Directions: Kids pretend to sing their favorite songs.

Magic Show

Materials: magic book, magic tricks and props as called for by book

Directions: Performing simple magic tricks can be another kind of performance that some kids find very appealing. It is crucial that kids have practiced beforehand to have the most success possible.

Pantomime

Materials: slips of paper, writing instrument(s), hat or container to draw slips of paper from

Directions: Kids can act out something they did earlier in the day or draw suggestions out of a hat of things to pantomime. Ideas should be active and simple - sports and some professions work well.

The Play's the Thing

Materials: book(s) of kid-oriented plays, props to use for plays

Directions: Kids love to create and perform their own simple plays as well as existing plays. Group time is an ideal time for such performances.

Puppet Show

Materials: puppets (can be homemade)

Directions: Kids can create their own puppets and stories to perform for everyone at group time.

Talent Show

Materials: depends on the act

Directions: This could be a major production or an impromptu opportunity for kids to share jokes or stories that they know. Some programs have a weekly talent day where kids perform songs, dances, or cheers or share jokes and stories.

Games

Here are some basic guidelines for games.

1. **They should not be competitive or team-based.** Games should focus on cooperation or taking turns instead of skills because in a school-age program there may be children from kindergarten through 6th grades playing together.

2. **Games for transition activities should be circle games or sit-down games.** Running games best suited to a gym or outdoor setting will not serve as effective transitions because the group will get wound up and need more time to play.

However, an active game within the boundaries of a circle may give kids a chance to burn off some energy. This may be necessary when kids have limited time for outdoor play.

3. **Games should be easy for children to join.** There should either be easy stopping and starting points in the game or it should be ongoing so that children can join in as they finish prior activities.

When considering games, look at those already familiar to you and consider how they could be changed to keep them fresh. Consider how you could develop variations for the following:

Duck Duck Goose   Heads Up Seven Up
Hot Potato   Limbo
Musical Chairs   Simon Says

You can also consider traditional small group games or partner games and how they could be adapted into games for larger groups during transition times:

Checkers   Connect 4™   Win, Lose, or Draw
Dominoes   Hangman
Outburst™   Tic Tac Toe

Here are some other games that work well for transitions:

All About Me

Materials: none

Directions: The group leader asks children questions about themselves. Questions might be "What is my last name?" "Middle name?" "Where was I born?" "What is my favorite color?"

This game can be used over and over because it gives children chances to learn about the adults and children in the group.

Contributed by: Emily Riddle, Site Facilitator at Derby Ridge Adventure Club in Columbia, MO.

Card Bingo

Materials: old decks of cards, hole punch, brads

Directions: This is a good way to use up old decks of cards. Take 5 playing cards, punch a hole in the corner, and clip them together with a brad. Make several sets and keep them in a bag or basket. The leader shuffles one complete deck of cards and then reads and shows cards one at a time. The players try to match that card to one of the five in their hands. When a child has all 5 cards matched, he/she gets a Bingo.

Contributed by: Kristi Fate, Assistant Coordinator at Kids Country Program in Lee's Summit, MO. Kristi got the idea from Janet Scarborough, Site Coordinator at Thomas Ultican Elementary's Prime Time program in Blue Springs, MO.

Circle Basketball

Materials: soft, spongy ball and a basket or container

Directions: Have kids take turns shooting the ball into a basket or other container. Children making a basket might get a turn to share something they brought or did that day.

Circle Time Games Box

Materials: box, index cards, writing instruments, necessary props

Directions: Keep instructions and props in a box for several games such as "Button, Button, Who's Got the Button?," "Doggy, Doggy, Where's Your Bone?," "Hot Potato," "Duck, Duck, Goose," and "Telephone." Write up instructions for the games and put them in the box along with the necessary props and you have an instant circle time games box.

Contributed by: Kristi Fate, Assistant Coordinator at Kids Country Program in Lee's Summit, MO.

Circle Volleyball

Materials: balloon

Directions: Kids sit in a circle and take turns batting a balloon to keep it in the air. Let the group keep track of how many times they hit the balloon before it touches the ground. Kids might also keep track of how many kids touch the balloon before it hits the ground.

Do What I Do

Materials: none

Directions: One person is sent out of the room. A child in the circle is picked as the leader. The child starts a motion and everyone else copies it. The person sent out of the room comes back in and tries to guess who the leader is.

Electricity

Materials: none

Directions: Kids hold hands. One person squeezes lightly to send the "electricity" around the circle. Kids pass it on to next person. You can change the speed or send several at once.

Follow the Leader

Materials: none

Directions: When waiting for the group to line up, the adult can lead the children around the room in a game of Follow the Leader until everyone has joined the line.

Contributed by: Matt Nelson from Lucy Franklin Elementary's Prime Time program in Blue Springs, MO.

Fruit Basket Upset

Materials: none

Directions: Children are divided into several groups of fruit. One child, the fruit fly, is in the middle. When the fruit fly calls out a fruit (let's say "apple"), all apples must change places. The fruit fly tries to take the place of one of the apples. Whoever is left is the fruit fly. If the fruit fly yells "Fruit basket upset!" then everyone switches places.

Guard the Castle

Materials: soft ball

Directions: One child (the guard) is in the middle and a can or object is placed under his/her legs. Kids in the circle roll the ball to try to knock down the guard's "castle." If successful, the child takes the guard's place in the center.

Going on a Trip to Mars

Materials: none

Directions: Tell children that there is a trick to this. When they figure it out, they should keep playing and NOT reveal the secret. This works best with older children (3rd and up).

The first person starts by saying her name and an object. For example, "my name is Elaine and I'm bringing eggs." The next person follows suit: "my name is Dave and I'm bringing dogs." The catch is that children must say an object that starts with the same letter as their names. If Gwen says, "I'm Gwen and I'm bringing cats," then the leader says, "I'm sorry, Gwen. You can't go."

There will always be a Sullivan who wants to bring dogs and questions why he can't if Dave can. Simply remind kids that there is a trick and to pay attention. The game can continue until all children catch on.

Contributed by: Elaine McGee, Missouri School-Age Care Coalition (MOSAC2) President 1999-2000.

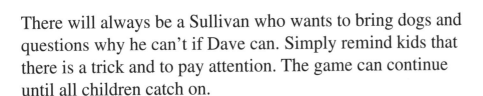

Hide and Seek

Materials: none

Directions: This is different from the traditional version. Only one child hides and one child seeks. The group can give clues (like indicating if seeker is hot or cold) to help seeker find hider. When found, the seeker becomes the new hider and the hider picks a new seeker.

Hot Potato

Materials: an object to be the potato, radio or tape/CD player

Directions: While music is playing, children pass the "hot potato" to each other. When the music stops, the child holding the potato is out. That child then works the music the next time around. Be sure that whoever does the music cannot see the rest of the group.

Contributed by: Elaine McGee, Missouri School-Age Care Coalition (MOSAC2) President 1999-2000.

The Hula Hoop Game

Materials: hula hoops

Directions: Children hold hands in a circle. Two kids lock hands through a hula hoop. When the hula hoop gets to each child, the child must pass through the hula hoop without breaking hands. For variations, add more hula hoops or have more than one child go through a hoop at a time.

In the Brook, On the Bank

Materials: none

Directions: Kids line up facing a leader. When the leader says "In the brook" everyone must jump to the left and when the leader says "On the bank" everyone must jump to the right. Leader can say "On the brook" or "In the bank" to trick people. The leader can also jump the wrong direction to throw people off. Last person left becomes new leader.

Line Up

Materials: none

Directions: Group is asked to line up based on, say, earliest birthdays (January) to latest birthdays (December). Children can also line up based on height, darkness or lightness of hair or shoes, etc. To make it even more challenging, children can be asked to line up without talking.

Contributed by: Elaine McGee, Missouri School-Age Care Coalition (MOSAC2) President 1999-2000.

Mum Ball

Materials: soft ball

Directions: Kids sit in circle, rolling a ball back and forth without speaking. Kids who speak are out. Kids could also get out for laughing, smiling, touching the ball with their hands, or other ideas dreamed up by the group. Kids who are out can become clowns to try to get others to laugh, speak, etc.

Nervous Breakdown

Materials: soft ball

Directions: Kids form a circle with one child (the doctor) in the middle. The kids must keep both hands behind their backs unless the ball is thrown to them. If they drop the ball or the doctor tricks them into thinking he/she is going to throw it, then they are out. The last child left becomes the new doctor.

Pinball

Materials: soft ball

Directions: All children turn their backs to the circle, bend over, and bat the ball back and forth to each other like a pinball machine.

Quiet As a Mouse

Materials: none

Directions: Kids may circulate or talk until the leader (the cat) yells "Quiet as a mouse!" Anyone the cat catches moving or talking is out. The last mouse becomes the new cat.

Relays

Materials: objects for passing

Directions: While standing in line, children can do relays. Children pass an object down the line in different ways (over the shoulder, under the legs, etc.).

Contributed by: Elaine McGee, Missouri School-Age Care Coalition (MOSAC2) President 1999-2000.

Telephone

Materials: none

Directions: A leader tells the first child a "secret" and that child whispers it to the next child. The message is passed on until everyone has heard it. The last person announces the message so that everyone can hear how different it is from the original message.

Contributed by: Ruth Driver from Cordill-Mason Elementary's Prime Time program in Blue Springs, MO.

Trivia

Materials: none necessary, but cards from a trivia game can be used

Directions: This is a great way for children to learn more about the adults as well as each other. The leader can ask the group trivia questions pertaining to herself ("How old am I?" "How tall am I?" "What is my middle name?") or use cards from an actual trivia game.

Contributed by: Emily Riddle, Site Facilitator at Derby Ridge Adventure Club in Columbia, MO.

Guessing Games

Am I in the Club?

Materials: none

Directions: One child (the Club Leader) stands in front of the group and picks a common characteristic of themselves and others sitting in the group (such as anyone wearing blue). Children ask the Club Leader, "Am I in the club?" The Club Leader responds "Yes" or "No" accordingly. The rest of the group tries to guess the common characteristics of the club members. The child who guesses right becomes the new Club Leader.

Contributed by: Christi Logan from James Walker Elementary's Prime Time program in Blue Springs, MO.

Button, Button, Who's Got the Button?

Materials: string, button

Directions: Put a string through the holes of a button and tie. The string should be long enough that all the kids can sit in a circle and grasp the string. Kids pass the button along the string trying to keep the child in the middle of the circle from seeing it. That child tries to figure out who has the button.

Contributed by: Elaine McGee, Missouri School-Age Care Coalition (MOSAC2) President, 1999-2000.

Doggy, Doggy, Where's Your Bone?

Materials: an object to be the bone

Directions: One person is the dog in the center of the circle. When the dog's eyes are closed, someone takes the dog's bone. Then everyone chants, "Doggy, doggy, where's your bone? Somebody stole it from your home. Guess who, maybe you!"

The dog opens his eyes and has three turns to guess who has the bone. If the dog guesses correctly, he gets another turn. If not, the person who had the bone becomes the new dog.

Eye Witness

Materials: none

Directions: One person stands up and everyone looks at her. She leaves the room and changes something about herself. (Example: she tucks in her shirt, removes her watch, etc.). When she returns to the room, the group guesses what the person changed. The person who guesses correctly gets the next turn.

Contributed by: Matt Nelson from Lucy Franklin's Prime Time program in Blue Springs, MO.

Guess Who

Materials: none

Directions: The person who is "It" thinks of someone else in the group. "It" offers one clue (such as, "This person is a boy" or "This person is wearing red," etc.) and the group has three tries to guess who has been chosen. If the group does not get it, "It' offers another clue. Play continues until someone guesses correctly. That person becomes the new "It."

Contributed by: Cindy Keeports, Assistant Site Coordinator from Chapel Lakes Elementary's Prime Time program in Blue Springs, MO.

Guess Who (Alternate Version)

Materials: none

Directions: The group can ask yes/no questions. ("Is this person a girl?" "Is this person wearing green?") to figure out who "It" is thinking of.

I'm Thinking Of...

Materials: none

Directions: The leader gazes around the room or area and says, "I'm thinking of something that..." (for example) "...is purple." Children guess what the leader is talking about. It has to be something everyone can see. It is more fun to pick objects of which there are multiples; then it is more challenging for kids to pick the right one.

Contributed by: Diane Yi, art teacher from Smithville School District in Smithville, MO.

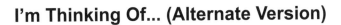

I'm Thinking Of... (Alternate Version)

Materials: none

Directions: To make the game more complicated, pick objects that children can't see. For example, "I'm thinking of something that starts with an 'S' that you can find in the night sky." (star) Kids can ask yes/no questions to get hints.

Contributed by: Elaine McGee, Missouri School-Age Care Coalition (MOSAC²) President, 1999-2000.

I Spy

Materials: none

Directions: The leader says, "I spy something with my eye that is the color green" (grass, leaves, flowers, etc.). The children guess until the correct object is found. The child who guesses correctly becomes the new "I Spy" leader. Note: the object must be something that everyone can actually see. However, the "I Spy" leader can be sneaky and avoid looking at the object to throw people off.

Contributed by: Cathy Zeysing, Reading Specialist in Blue Springs School District in Blue Springs, MO.

The Number Game

Materials: none

Directions: There are several possibilities here. The leader picks a number within a certain range and the other kids guess to see who can get closest. The leader could also pick a number and then as children guess, the leader tells them "higher" or "lower." The person guessing the number correctly becomes the new leader.

Contributed by: Jamie Martin from Daniel Young Elementary's Prime Time program in Blue Springs, MO.

Pass Out

Materials: objects for guessing

Directions: This is a lot like "Button, Button, Who's Got the Button?" One child gets an object. The next child who arrives tries to guess what the object is. The object could be a hint at what the upcoming activity of the day is. When that child guesses it, she gets to give clues to the next child that arrives.

Contributed by: Bill Turner from James Walker Elementary's Prime Time program in Blue Springs, MO.

Twenty Questions

Materials: none

Directions: Set this up as a quiz where the leader allows players to ask 20 yes/no questions to determine what she is thinking about. Questions could pertain to an activity or theme from the day/week.

Contributed by: Heather Amos from Cordill-Mason Elementary's Prime Time program in Blue Springs, MO.

Twenty Questions (Alternate Version)

Materials: none

Directions: One child leaves the room. When he returns, he asks up to 20 yes/no questions to determine which child was picked while he was out of the room.

Who's Missing?

Materials: none

Directions: One child closes his eyes. Another child secretly hides. First child gets three guesses to determine who's missing.

The Yes/No Game

Materials: none

Directions: The "Questioner" asks questions that can be answered "yes" or "no." Kids sit down when the answer is no and stand up when the answer is yes. You may opt to limit the number of questions per Questioner before someone else gets a turn.

Group Creations

These are projects that can be done in a group time setting that you normally might think of only during project time or free time. These can be wonderful opportunities to get the creative juices of the entire group flowing.

Building

Materials: blocks and/or other building material

Directions: Give each child a chance to add to a group building. It might be a small creation with blocks from the building area. It could be a large project involving rearrangement of some furniture to create a temporary house or other structure.

Collage

Materials: variety of art materials and interesting objects

Directions: Let each child add an object to a group collage. Objects could be attached to paper or poster board with glue or tape to make a permanent collage or objects can be arranged in a designated area to create a temporary collage. The collage might represent a theme or concept or be a spur-of-the-moment art creation.

Dot Picture

Materials: paper and writing instrument

Directions: The first person adds a dot on a piece of paper. The next person adds another dot. This continues until each person has at least one turn. As people add dots, they will eventually start to create an image or picture. Kids can title it and post it for everyone to see.

Contributed by: Dawn Butler from Chapel Lakes Elementary's Prime Time program in Blue Springs, MO.

Group Picture or Mural

Materials: paper, easel or blackboard along with appropriate writing materials

Directions: Pass a piece of paper around the room. Each child adds a detail to the picture. If possible, post the picture on an easel or blackboard where everyone will be able to see it as children add to it.

Letters/Thank You Notes and Cards

Materials: stationery, cards, writing material, envelopes, stamps, necessary addresses

Directions: You could be pen pals with another SAC program and write a letter as a group to them. Consider writing letters to celebrities or people in the community. This can also be an opportunity for writing thank you notes to parents, family members, or people in the school and community who have done something special for the group.

Map Making

Materials: paper and writing materials, rulers, tape measures, compasses

Directions: Let the kids make a group map of the room, the outside area, the school, your neighborhood, etc. Use the same approach as with doing a group picture or mural.

Mummy

Materials: several rolls of toilet paper, camera

Directions: Wrap the entire group in toilet paper to create a big mummy. This can also be done as a relay with teams racing to wrap one person in toilet paper. Be sure to get pictures.

Spider Web

Materials: ball of yarn

Directions: Children sit in a circle. One person holds on to the end of a ball of yarn and tosses the ball to someone on the opposite side of the circle. That person follows suit. By the time everyone has a hold of part of the yarn, a huge spider web has been formed!

Contributed by: Elaine McGee, Missouri School-Age Care Coalition (MOSAC²) President, 1999-2000.

Under Construction

Materials: blocks and other building materials

Directions: In an out-of-the-way area where it won't be disturbed, have an ongoing structure to which children can add. As children pass by, they can add something to the new building.

Contributed by: Dawn Butler from Chapel Lakes Elementary's Prime Time program in Blue Springs, MO.

Language

While children have plenty of exposure to language-oriented activities during the school day, there is still room in the be-fore-and-after school setting to do fun, language-oriented transition activities. Here are some ideas:

Get Off My Back!

Materials: none

Directions: If touching is not a problem, children can trace letters or numbers on each other's backs. They can guess what letter or number is being drawn. This can be done in a line with each person tracing a number or letter on the person's back in front of them. When everyone is finished, the line can turn around and face the other way and repeat the activity.

Contributed by: Elaine McGee, Missouri School-Age Care Coalition (MOSAC²) President, 1999-2000.

I Spy

Materials: none

Directions: "I Spy" can be played by finding words that begin with a particular letter or words that rhyme with other words. Example: "I spy something with my eye that starts with the letter 'B.'" (bat, ball, bus, etc.) "I spy something with my eye that rhymes with fly." (sky)

Contributed by: Cathy Zeysing, Reading Specialist from Blue Springs School District in Blue Springs, MO.

Reading Buddies

Materials: books

Directions: For a regular transition time (like cleaning up in the mornings and getting ready to go to school), older children can be paired with younger children and be their "Reading Buddies." During this time, older children can read books to younger ones.

Contributed by: Annette Schmitt, Adventure Club Site Facilitator from Columbia, MO.

Reading Time

Materials: books

Directions: An adult can read a story to children while they are waiting for others. A child could also read to the group or children can take turns. Depending on the size of the group, children might break into smaller groups.

Real or Make Believe?

Materials: none

Directions: The leader tells a story of which parts are real and parts are make believe. At the end, children guess which parts are which.

Sign Language

Materials: sign language book

Directions: The leader can sign letters or words to children and they guess them. This works especially well when walking down the hall. The leader can sign children's names to see if they can guess whose name was spelled.

Contributed by: Matt Nelson from Lucy Franklin Elementary's Prime Time program in Blue Springs, MO.

Silly Combination Stories

Materials: at least two different story books

Directions: The leader begins reading one book and then abruptly switches midstream to the other book to create a silly disjointed story. Depending on time, children can discuss what they thought would happen in the last half of the first story and the first half of the second story.

Spell-O-Rama

Materials: none

Directions: The adult offers up a word (let's say "environment") and the first child in line begins spelling it by only saying the first letter (so child would say "e"). The next child in line says "n" (hopefully) and this continues until the entire word is spelled or a child says an incorrect letter. The next word picks up from there.

Contributed by: Diane Yi, art teacher from Smithville School District in Smithville, MO.

Stories Told and Retold

Materials: slips of paper, writing instruments

Directions: Children are given a category such as animals, numbers, colors, sizes, or names. They can write things to fit that category on the slips of paper (only one item on each slip). These slips can then be used to replace objects in a story. For example, when reading "The Three Little Pigs," kids might draw new slips of paper that turn the story into "The 30,000 Giant Aardvarks."

Story Building

Materials: none

Directions: Each child adds a sentence to a story. This continues until all children have added a sentence or the story comes to a natural conclusion.

Contributed by: Dawn Butler from Chapel Lakes Elementary's Prime Time program in Blue Springs, MO.

Storytelling

Materials: none

Directions: The adult can tell a story to the children or children can make up stories for each other.

What Is It?

Materials: unusual objects that children have probably not seen before

Directions: An unusual object is introduced to the children. They in turn make up stories about how the object might be used.

What's in a Word?

Materials: none

Directions: One child offers a word that will be the theme. Let's say the child says "cat." The next child offers a word that starts with the last letter of the previous word. The catch is that the word must fit within the theme. For example, since "cat" ends with "t," the next child must offer a word that starts with "t" and is some kind of cat. That child might say "tiger." Play continues until a child is stumped.

Contributed by: Cathy Zeysing, Reading Specialist from Blue Springs School District in Blue Springs, MO.

Who Dunnit

Materials: none

Directions: For older children, a mystery-solving game can be made out of "Twenty Questions." Children can even be taught the elements of story and problem-solving skills.

The leader imagines a crime that has been committed. Children then have to guess what happened, where it happened, and "who dunnit." Example: let's say that the stapler has been stolen from the art area by Alicia (just for pretend!). Children then ask yes/no questions to determine what happened. This game can also be simplified to have children just figure out part of the crime. Example: tell children that the stapler has been stolen from the art area and they must figure out "who dunnit."

Math and Science

Like language-oriented activities, math and science can be incorporated into before-and-after-school programs in such a way as to give children different experiences than what they receive during the school day. Here are some possibilities:

Everyone Counts

Materials: none

Directions: Kids can count backwards or by 2s, 5s, etc. Kids can also count in other languages. This could be used for walking down the hall or waiting in line.

Contributed by: Matt Nelson from Lucy Franklin Elementary's Prime Time program in Blue Springs, MO.

Math Problems

Materials: none

Directions: When children are moving from one activity to another, ask simple math problems. Children can hold up the correct number of fingers to give the answer. The leader can walk down the line and high five the kids.

Contributed by: Jenne Buffington, a former kindergarten teacher and now Curriculum Writer for La Petite Corporation; Overland Park, KS.

Math Problems (Alternate Version)

Materials: none

Directions: When dismissing children, use math problems. Example: "If you are 6 + 2 years old, then you may go. If you are 20 - 13, then you may go."

Contributed by: Dawn Butler from Chapel Lakes Elementary's Prime Time program in Blue Springs, MO.

Science Experiments

Materials: tools for experimenting, books of simple science experiments

Directions: While science experiments are generally considered to be small group projects done more formally, some of them would work very well for total group experiences.

Sizing Up the Animal Kingdom

Materials: book that indicates the weight and height of animals, rulers or tape measures, string, tape, writing instruments, scale, paper

Directions: Let children guess how long, how tall or how heavy various animals are. For example, ask the children how tall they think a giraffe is. Mark off a starting line from which children walk as far as they think the giraffe is tall. Children stand in their spots until everyone guesses. Then measure off the actual height of the giraffe to see who is closest.

Weather Chart

Materials: graph paper, writing instruments, access to phone

Directions: Let kids guess what the temperature is outside. Record guesses. Then have someone call to find out the actual temperature or look it up on the Internet.

Music and Movement

Unfortunately, it would require another whole book to provide you with music and lyrics for all the songs listed in this section (not to mention a few copyright issues). However, you may know more songs than you think. Consider the camp songs, TV themes, and other silly songs that you knew as a child. This section provides a list of some of those songs in the hopes that they will jog your memory and you'll be able to share these songs with the kids.

One more note - songs are great for any kind of transition.

Songs

Along Came Herman the Worm

The Ants Go Marching

The Bear Song (the other day, I saw a bear...)

Beetle Jaws

Beverly Hillbillies

Bingo

The Brady Bunch

Down by the Bay

Father Abraham

The Flintstones

Found a Peanut

Frosty the Snowman

Gilligan's Island

Going on a Bear Hunt

The Grand Old Duke of York

Green Acres

The Green Grass Grows All Around

Here Comes Peter Cottontail

I Like Bananas, Coconuts, and Grapes

I'm a Little Bar of Soap

I'm a Little Pile of Tin

I'm a Little Teapot

The Jetsons

Songs, continued

Jimmy Crack Corn
Jingle Bells
Little Bunny Foo-Foo
Little Cabin in the Woods
Miss Suzie Had a Steamboat
My Bonnie Lies Over the Ocean
Old MacDonald Had a Farm
Peanut Butter
Peanut Sitting on a Railroad Track
Ring Around the Rosie
Row, Row, Row Your Boat
Rudolph the Red-Nosed Reindeer
Santa Claus Is Coming to Town
Who Stole the Cookie from the Cookie Jar?
Yankee Doodle
You're a Grand Old Flag
Zip-a-Dee-Doo-Dah

Keep the following ideas in mind for rejuvenating familiar songs.

- Sing faster or slower or alternate speeds.
- Sing louder or softer or alternate volumes.
- Sing the song in an exaggerated tone such as extra silly or extra serious.
- Add gestures.
- Sing in different styles (rock, opera, blues, rap, lounge act).
- Write new words.
- Act out song.
- Combine any of the above.

In addition to singing songs and finding ways to reinvent them, consider these music and movement-oriented activities for transition times:

Aerobics/Exercise

Materials: radio or CD/tape player

Directions: Don't overdo it or kids think of it as work, but it can be fun to let one of the kids lead the group in an exercise or two. Turn on the radio or CD/tape player and let kids make up their own aerobics.

Brown Bear, Brown Bear, What Do You See?

Materials: none

Directions: Based on the book of the same name. The leader begins, for example, "Kaitlin, Kaitlin, what do you see?"

Kaitlin responds, "I see a _____ looking at me" and then continues to the next person.

This continues down the line with the blank being filled in by the actual story, children's names, animals, or anything else you choose.

Contributed by: Diane Yi, art teacher from Smithville School District in Smithville, MO.

Clap in Rhythm

Materials: none

Directions: Let one person start a clapping rhythm and then everyone else copies it.

Contributed by: Elaine McGee, Missouri School-Age Care Coalition (MOSAC[2]) President, 1999-2000.

Data Disco

Materials: none

Directions: Children waiting to go to the next activity do a side-to-side two step and answer questions to the rhythm. This can be done either with or without music.

Contributed by: Diane Yi, art teacher from Smithville School District in Smithville, MO.

A Hush Fell Over the Crowd

Materials: none

Directions: When you need the attention of children who are already relatively controlled but increasing in noise level, make a large sweeping gesture with your hands as you say "And a hussssssh fell over the crowd." This is the children's cue to respond with a "husssssh."

Contributed by: Emily Riddle, Site Facilitator at Derby Ridge Adventure Club in Columbia, MO.

Laryngitis Singing

Materials: none

Directions: Choose a song that everyone knows. On the count of three, everyone starts singing, but without any noise! At different points the leader can give a sign and everyone sings out loud again to see where everyone is at in the song. This is a great activity for walking down halls - everyone can break into song upon their arrival at the final destination.

Contributed by: Jenne Buffington, former kindergarten teacher and now Curriculum Writer for La Petite Corporation in Overland Park, KS.

The Rainstorm

Materials: none

Directions: This works best if all kids are sitting in a circle. The leader slowly points her finger at the kids, moving around the circle until she has pointed toward everyone. On the first wave, children rub their hands together when they are pointed at. On subsequent waves they will snap, clap, slap their legs, and stomp their feet. The leader then does the whole thing in reverse.

A Step in Time

Materials: none

Directions: The leader starts a steady beat by snapping, tapping, clapping or using a musical instrument. The children keep the beat by stepping back and forth from left to right. The leader can also sound out various rhythm patterns for the children to repeat back.

Contributed by: Cathy Zeysing, Reading Specialist from Blue Springs District in Blue Springs, MO.

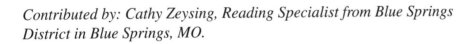

Planning

Any time you have a few extra moments, you can get children's input on program ideas. Planning makes for an excellent transition activity, especially for "set" transitions or "ready" transitions.

If you decide to do this in a circle or gathering time, keep these tips in mind:

1. **Keep it brief.** Kids will get bored "just sitting there."

2. **Give as many kids as possible a chance for suggestions.** Kids will get frustrated if they don't feel like they have a voice.

3. **Let kids know when you will stop soliciting ideas.** Give it a set time or say something like "We'll go around the circle one more time and give each person a chance to make one last suggestion."

4. **Write down kids' ideas.** They will know that you are taking them seriously.

Here are some possibilities for planning:
- Suggestions for circle time activities
- Suggestions for activity time ideas
- Suggestions for new materials to add to areas
- Suggestions for new outdoor materials
- Ideas for creating a new area
- Brainstorming for special projects
- Brainstorming ideas for full and half days

Sharing

Sharing should be a time for kids to talk about what they have done at school, in their SAC program, or at home. It might be something they did that day, that weekend, or last summer. They may have specific interests or actual objects they wish to share with the group. Your program may opt to regularly incorporate sharing times into your program.

In any event, sharing works well for any kind of transition. Here are some possible questions for initiating sharing:

- What area did you play in today?
- What did you play with today?
- Who did you play with today?
- Who went to the art area today? What did you do there?
- What was the neatest thing you did in school today?
- What did you do last weekend?
- What are you going to do this weekend?
- What is something you are looking forward to?
- What is your favorite food?
- What is your favorite movie?

- What is your favorite book?
- What is your favorite color?
- Anyone who has a birthday in October may share.
- Anyone whose first name starts with the letter "A" may share.
- Anyone wearing the color purple may share.
- Anyone with brown hair may share.
- Roll a ball to someone. Whoever holds the ball shares and then rolls it to someone else.
- Tie a care to a string and roll it to someone.
- Roll a ball of yarn to someone. After sharing, wrap the yarn around your foot and then roll it to someone else.

NOTES